Original title:
Enjoy the Little Things

Copyright © 2024 Book Fairy Publishing
All rights reserved.

Editor: Theodor Taimla
Author: Isabella Ilves
ISBN HARDBACK: 978-9916-763-20-9
ISBN PAPERBACK: 978-9916-763-21-6

Gentle Rejoicing

Beneath the sky, we softly tread,
Where tender whispers gently spread.
In fields of dreams, our spirits fly,
Each breath a song that heaves a sigh.

The gentle rain, a soft embrace,
Like teardrops on a quiet face.
Amidst the calm, a heart does lift,
In gentle storms, we find our gift.

Morning light, a soft caress,
Gracing all with tenderness.
Birds in chorus, sweet and pure,
Love revealed in whispers sure.

Everyday Bliss

Sunrise spills its golden rays,
Heralding the start of days.
Mornings filled with fragrant steam,
Coffee cups and daylight's gleam.

Laughter shared in simple things,
Joy that simple life can bring.
Moments caught in fleeting jest,
Find contentment; it's the best.

Daily tasks and humble chores,
Open unsuspecting doors.
Love and care in worked-out hands,
This is where true life expands.

Tiny Sparks of Joy

In the hush of evening's glow,
Tiny sparks begin to show.
Fireflies with gentle light,
Turning darkness into sight.

A whispered breeze, a child's laugh,
Two hearts chart a shared path.
In twinkle lights of silent nights,
Soft reveries and pure delights.

Within each day, these sparks reside,
Moments where our joys abide.
Simple acts with hearts imbued,
Tiny sparks of gratitude.

Everyday Bliss

Sunrise spills its golden rays,
Heralding the start of days.
Mornings filled with fragrant steam,
Coffee cups and daylight's gleam.

Laughter shared in simple things,
Joy that simple life can bring.
Moments caught in fleeting jest,
Find contentment; it's the best.

Daily tasks and humble chores,
Open unsuspecting doors.
Love and care in worked-out hands,
This is where true life expands.

Tiny Sparks of Joy

In the hush of evening's glow,
Tiny sparks begin to show.
Fireflies with gentle light,
Turning darkness into sight.

A whispered breeze, a child's laugh,
Two hearts chart a shared path.
In twinkle lights of silent nights,
Soft reveries and pure delights.

Within each day, these sparks reside,
Moments where our joys abide.
Simple acts with hearts imbued,
Tiny sparks of gratitude.

Smiles in Small Places

A neighbor's wave, a friendly nod,
Seen in spaces, paths are trod.
A fleeting grin, a shared delight,
Brightens moments, night or light.

A flower's bloom, unexpected,
In garden paths, joy reflected.
Eyes that meet and quickly smile,
Make the world seem less hostile.

In smallest places, joy is found,
Hearts and spirits are unbound.
Smiles exchanged along the way,
Guide us through an endless day.

Little Joys

In the whisper of the breeze,
Through the rustle of the leaves,
Find the secrets life conceives,
Little joys, like hidden keys.

In the laughter of a child,
In a day's work reconciled,
See the world with vision mild,
In little joys, be beguiled.

Big Smiles

Beneath a sky of endless blue,
In a world both old and new,
Find the moments to construe,
Big smiles waiting just for you.

In the heart's sincere embrace,
In a friend's familiar face,
Feel the warmth time can't erase,
Big smiles light up every space.

Echoes of Bliss

In the morning's gentle rise,
Through the twilight's soft goodbyes,
Echoes flutter through the skies,
Bliss unspoken never dies.

In each whisper heard and missed,
Cast in shadows by the mist,
Moments shared in love persist,
Echoes of bliss softly kissed.

Fleeting Wonders

In the dawn's first tender light,
In the stars that pierce the night,
Wonders fleeting, pure and bright,
Spark a moment's sweet delight.

In the fleeting waves that roll,
In the stories yet untold,
Capture wonders, purest gold,
Fleeting moments warm the soul.

Heart's Ease

In the quiet of the morn,
Through the fields where life is born,
Ease the heart, away from scorn,
Find the peace for which we yearn.

In the notes of songs unsung,
In the tales of old and young,
Ease the heart, where dreams have clung,
Find the peace that's always sung.

Gentle Rhythms

Waves that kiss the shore with grace,
Softly humming, time they trace.
Moonlight dances on the sea,
Lulling hearts in harmony.

Whispers carried on the breeze,
Echoes of the silent seas.
Stars above, a sparkling dome,
Guiding wanderers back home.

Night's embrace, so calm, so deep,
Cradles dreams where angels sleep.
Oceans sing their lullabies,
Underneath the twilight skies.

Evening's Hush

Twilight falls, a velvet shroud,
Drawing stillness from the crowd.
Crickets start their evening tune,
Underneath the rising moon.

Whispers of the dying day,
Blend with stars in soft display.
Breezes waltz through leaves so fine,
Cooling earth in sacred time.

Shadows stretch, but do not fright,
Guardians of the approaching night.
Peace descends, in gentle rush,
Wrapped in evening's tender hush.

Maple Leaf Whispers

Leaves that flutter, whispering low,
Stories of the winds that blow.
Autumn's breath in colors bright,
Painting woods with sheer delight.

Branches sway in rhythmic song,
Echoing where whispers throng.
Sunset gleams through crimson veil,
Coating paths in amber trail.

Listen close to nature's lore,
Maple leaves have tales in store.
Every rustle, every sigh,
Secrets shared beneath the sky.

Threads of Gold

Sunlight streams through morning dew,
Weaving gold in patterns new.
Threads of dawn in golden hue,
Wake the world with promises true.

Meadows bask in gilded rays,
Flowers turn in silent praise.
Birdsong sparks the waking air,
As if life itself were a prayer.

Moments spun in threads of gold,
Stories of the days of old.
Every beam a silent thread,
Joining past where dreams are fed.

Echoes of Joy

In morning's light, the skies unfold,
With hues of blue and clouds of gold.
Birds sing melodies, pure and bright,
Echoes of joy in the dawn's first light.

Children's laughter fills the air,
A timeless gift, beyond compare.
The world awakes in radiant cheer,
Joy's echoes whisper, far and near.

In every heart, a spark resides,
A beacon shining, as time glides.
Hold close this joy, both far and near,
Echoes of happiness, crystal clear.

Tiny Sparks of Wonder

In a dew-kissed garden, petals gleam,
Whispers of wonders in dawn's soft beam.
Tiny insects dance, unseen yet bright,
In every shadow, a spark of light.

The stars at night, in silent grace,
Trace ancient paths through endless space.
Tiny sparks weave stories in the dark,
Each point a whisper, each moment stark.

In a child's gaze, pure and deep,
A world of wonder softly creeps.
Embrace the moments, small yet grand,
Tiny sparks of wonder, close at hand.

Hidden Gemstones

Beneath the earth, in shadows deep,
Lie treasures hidden, secrets keep.
Gemstones glimmer, unseen by day,
In silent darkness, they softly sway.

Through life's trails, we seek and find,
Hidden treasures, both heart and mind.
In quiet moments, truths unfold,
Hidden gemstones, precious, bold.

In every soul, a gem does lie,
A spark of light beneath the sky.
Seek within, let wonders shine,
Hidden gemstones, pure, divine.

Grace in the Ordinary

In the morning brew, a simple joy,
A touch of warmth, no vast employ.
A reaching hand, a shared embrace,
There lies the beauty, humble grace.

The rustling leaves, a calm serenade,
A gentle breeze, an earthy parade.
In daily life, where moments blend,
Grace in the ordinary, without end.

Through mundane tasks, a silent song,
In every step, we grow strong.
Find the grace in paths we trace,
Ordinary moments, a gentle embrace.

Miracles in a Moment

In the whisper of the breeze,
A world of wonders hides,
Miracles unseen by eyes,
Yet felt within our ties.

A fleeting glance, a touch,
Time pauses, transcends space,
In the heartbeat of the hush,
Eternity we trace.

Stars that shimmer in the night,
They tell of ancient lore,
In a moment's twinkling light,
Timeless tales they pour.

Miracles in a moment's grace,
Unfold like secret wings,
In silent skies, they embrace,
Simple, sacred things.

Simple Gratifications

Morning's golden ray of light,
Kissing gently sleepy skies,
Birds that sing with pure delight,
Nature's gentle lullabies.

A smile from a passing heart,
Warms the soul with tender flames,
Simple joys, they play their part,
In life's intricate games.

The scent of flowers in the air,
Blossoms painting fields anew,
Gratitude found everywhere,
In shades of every hue.

Hands that hold and hearts that care,
Love's unspoken, endless chase,
Moments shared beyond compare,
Time and space embrace.

Pebbles of Peace

By the shore where dreams reside,
Pebbles whisper soft and low,
In their stillness, oceans hide,
Tales of ebb and flow.

In each pebble lies a prayer,
Crafted by the hand of time,
Silent echoes in the air,
Gentle, graceful rhyme.

Waves that kiss the silent sand,
Hold a truth in every crest,
Peace, they offer with each hand,
Lullaby of rest.

Pebbles of peace, serene and small,
Speak of journeys we embark,
In their presence, we stand tall,
Lighting up the dark.

Soft Laughter

Soft laughter in the dim-lit room,
Echoes warm with gentle grace,
Banishing the growing gloom,
Lighting up each face.

A ripple through the silent air,
Touching hearts with tender sound,
Binding souls without a care,
Unity profound.

Chasing shadows from the night,
Laughter's dance, a fleeting ghost,
In its wake, purest light,
Moments we love most.

Soft laughter like a melody,
Sings of joy so pure and true,
In its cadence, we are free,
Life begins anew.

Sunset Silhouettes

Golden hues caress the skies,
Whispering secrets to the night.
Shadows dance in soft goodbyes,
Yielding to the fading light.

Twilight paints the world in gray,
Stars igniting, one and all.
Nature's end, a grand ballet,
To the moon's hypnotic call.

Waves reflect the coral's gleam,
Brushing shores with velvet hands.
Daytime slips into a dream,
Life unwinds on tranquil sands.

Euphoric Echoes

Laughter ripples through the air,
Joy abounds without a trace.
Euphoria beyond compare,
Written on each smiling face.

Music swells and hearts collide,
Drowning worries in delight.
Miracles do not hide,
In the day and in the night.

Moments rise in blissful arcs,
Leaving trails of warmth behind.
Euphoric echoes, gentle sparks,
Imprinted on the mind.

Quiet Jubilations

Whispers of a gentle breeze,
Celebrate the silent morn.
Nature's quiet symphonies,
With the dawn are gently born.

Leaves applaud the coming light,
Rustling in a soft embrace.
Quiet jubilations bright,
Dawning on the earth's own grace.

Birdsongs weave a subtle thread,
Through the tapestry of dawn.
In the shade of amber red,
Life's serenades are drawn.

Subtle Celebrations

In the pulse of daily strife,
Tiny triumphs pave the way.
Subtle celebrations rife,
With the bloom of each new day.

Unseen victories take flight,
In the hush of quiet grace.
Candles flicker through the night,
Casting warmth across the space.

Moments small but deeply felt,
Every tear a silent song.
In the heart where memories dwell,
Subtle celebrations strong.

Heartfelt Halcyon

In the quiet, whispers dance,
Underneath the twilight's glance.
Dreams of peace in amber glow,
Where the tranquil rivers flow.

Sunsets melt in hues of gold,
Stories of the heart unfold.
Waves of grace and calm embrace,
Carving paths in endless space.

Stars ignite the evening's song,
Carrying our souls along.
Through the night, a gentle sigh,
Harmonies that never die.

Winds caress the fields of time,
Chasing echoes most sublime.
In this heartfelt halcyon,
Lives the love we lean upon.

Little Joy Journeys

Every moment holds a chance,
In a playful, vibrant dance.
Little joys in every sight,
Painted with pure delight.

Dancing leaves and morning dew,
Smiles that linger, always new.
Steps we take in curious grace,
Guided by a warm embrace.

Laughs that echo through the air,
In a world that's free from care.
Balloons that rise, dreams that fly,
Underneath the boundless sky.

Candles flicker in the night,
Whispers shared by soft moonlight.
Tiny sparks of happiness,
Lighting up our life's recess.

Seeds of Serenity

In the garden of the mind,
Seeds of peace we're sure to find.
Silent growth beneath the earth,
Whispers of a second birth.

Morning light on petals fair,
Breathes the soul's unspoken prayer.
Blossoms stretch with gentle ease,
Swaying in the summer breeze.

Rays of gold and skies so blue,
Harmony in every hue.
Every leaf and every stem,
Rings a nature's quiet gem.

Rest in moments softly shared,
In this sanctuary spared.
Serenity in every vein,
In the gentle summer rain.

Faith in Finites

In the world of fleeting days,
Find the hope in subtle ways.
Finite moments softly blend,
Into stories without end.

Stars that fade and suns that rise,
Life within the compromise.
In each heartbeat, in each glance,
Lives a world of second chance.

Paths that twist and trails that wind,
All we've lost and all we find.
Cherish every tender thread,
Woven in the lives we've led.

In the finite, find the whole,
In each piece, a part of soul.
Faith in moments brief and bright,
Guides us through the endless night.

Stardust Moments

Beneath the velvet skies, dreams take their flight,
In whispers of the night, stars share their light,
Eons of wishes trace the milky way,
In stardust moments, time begins to sway.

A comet's embrace on paths we've yet to see,
Galactic tales of what could never be,
Ephemeral glows paint the cosmos bright,
In stardust moments, love ignites the night.

Constellations form in a celestial dance,
Ethereal silence, an endless trance,
In stardust moments, hearts start to glean,
The universe whispers, pure and serene.

Tiny Miracles

In petals' bloom, a world anew,
Raindrops sparkling, morning's dew,
Life's smallest moments, soft and kind,
In tiny miracles, treasures we find.

The flutter of wings, a gentle breeze,
Whispers of nature among the trees,
In every heartbeat, a story untold,
In tiny miracles, wonders unfold.

A baby's laughter, pure and bright,
Glimmering stars lighting the night,
In tender touches of everyday grace,
In tiny miracles, joy finds its place.

Embers in the Cold

In winter's embrace, the fire still glows,
Embers in the cold, warmth slowly shows,
Whispers of the past in flickering light,
In memories' glow, we hold the night.

Beneath the frost, dreams start to ignite,
Hope kindles softly, banishing fright,
In shadows long, our stories unfold,
Embers in the cold, tales softly told.

Amidst the silence, a promise kept,
In embers' glow, where wishes are swept,
Through icy darkness, spirits behold,
A spark of courage, embers in the cold.

Harmony of Hues

Colors merging, a canvas so wide,
In harmony of hues, dreams coincide,
Each stroke whispers, a tale to be,
Brushing life into artistry.

Sunset's palette, soft and grand,
In every hue, a guiding hand,
Nature's orchestra, vibrant, free,
Creating symphonies, a sight to see.

In twilight's mix, where shadows merge,
A song of colors on the verge,
In harmony of hues, hearts align,
Painting moments, yours and mine.

Cherishing Quietude

In the hush of morning light,
Whispers of the dawn unfurl,
Silence drapes the world in white,
Moments pure, a hidden pearl.

Leaves that rustle, softly speak,
Echoes of an ancient song,
In their dance, a silence sleek,
Nature's pause, serene and long.

Glimmers of a tranquil day,
In the gentle brook's embrace,
Stillness in the hearts that play,
Peace reflects in every face.

Eve descends, the night prevails,
Stars ignite the velvet skies,
Quietude in twilight's trails,
Calm unfolds where silence lies.

Cherish now the muted sound,
In the heart, a silent prayer,
In the quiet, dreams are found,
Voice of peace, beyond compare.

Fleeting Elation

A whisper, then a roar inside,
Heartbeats race, the moment's grand,
Joy's a wave, a sparkling tide,
Summoned by an unseen hand.

In your eyes, a flash of light,
Smiles that burst in pure delight,
Elation's wings, they lift in flight,
Through the day and through the night.

Laughter ripples, breaks the day,
Color bleeds through every hue,
Sunlight dances, shadows play,
Life's a canvas, bright and new.

Clouds burst open, rainbows arch,
In the storm, a gleaming part,
Fleeting moments, on they march,
Joy seared deeply in the heart.

Catch these glimmers, hold them dear,
Transient though they often be,
Every fleeting moment near,
Marks a life eternally.

Ripples of Joy

In the pond of day's repose,
Ripples play, the surface bright,
Every stone a joy that throws,
Circles spread in pure delight.

Laughter lightens air and time,
Echoes of a happy past,
Moments pass in joyous rhyme,
Memories are made to last.

Gleaming eyes that meet and share,
Hindered not by weary days,
Joyful ripples everywhere,
Linger in the heart's vast bays.

Hands that clasp in warmth and cheer,
Words that fill the empty spaces,
Ripples stretch beyond mere here,
Binding hearts in countless places.

Let each ripple be a song,
Sung in every heart anew,
Joyful notes, transcending long,
Ripples dance in skies so blue.

Unseen Delights

In the whispers of the breeze,
Secrets of the unseen world,
Mysteries unfold with ease,
Magic in its arms unfurled.

Flowers bloom where none have looked,
Stars that shine beyond the night,
Miracles in shadows, tucked,
Wonders hidden from our sight.

Eyes that see the common day,
Often miss what lies beneath,
Unseen joys in mundane play,
Beauties wrapped in nature's sheath.

Whispers of a soul untouched,
Dreams that hide within our ken,
Delights unseen, but known and clutched,
By the hearts and souls of men.

Cherish what remains to find,
In the silent, graced nights,
In the unseen, joy and mind,
Merge in quiet, pure delights.

Beneath the Dappled Light

Beneath the dappled light we lay,
Soft whispers in the breezes play,
The leaves above, a fragile veil,
In nature's arms, we softly sail.

The sunbeam dances through the green,
A fleeting kiss, a golden scene,
With every shade, our dreams ignite,
A canvas painted with delight.

The world outside fades to a blur,
In stillness, hearts begin to stir,
A symphony in hush conceals,
The unspoken truths that love reveals.

In twilight's tender embrace,
Time slows, as fingers interlace,
Stars above, a distant choir,
Echoing our quiet fire.

Moments pass, yet linger sweet,
In memories where time retreats,
In dappled light, we find our peace,
A gentle love that will not cease.

Evergreen Memories

Beneath the firs, we find our way,
Where time stands still, and echoes play,
In evergreens, our secrets keep,
A forest deep where shadows leap.

The scent of pine, a fragrant spell,
Of stories only hearts can tell,
In whispered winds, our voices blend,
In nature's arms, we find our friend.

Footsteps fall on needles soft,
In teal and jade, our memories loft,
The canopy, a shelter sure,
Of love and life, so deep, so pure.

The sun through boughs, a gentle hue,
A touch of warmth, a sky of blue,
Amidst the green, our spirits soar,
In silent joy, we are restored.

The echoes of a time that's past,
In stillness, we find peace at last,
Evergreen whispers call us home,
In nature's heart, we're not alone.

Sunlight on Your Face

The sunlight on your face does play,
Caressing softly, golden ray,
In every smile, a story told,
Of love that never would grow old.

Your eyes, they sparkle with the dawn,
As morning breaks and shadows yawn,
A new day blooms within their light,
And promises the stars at night.

Your laughter floats on gentle air,
A melody that's beyond compare,
In every glance, a dance ensues,
A song of life, in varied hues.

The world around begins to glow,
As if in awe of what you show,
The sun, it finds a kindred soul,
In you, the light is made whole.

In moments brief, yet endless too,
The sunlight brings me close to you,
A warmth that lingers and embraces,
In every touch, a love retraces.

Harmonies in Silence

In silence, where the heartbeats lie,
Unspoken words beneath the sky,
A symphony without a sound,
Where whispered truths and love abound.

The quiet hum of thoughts entwined,
In stillness, peace is gently mined,
With every pause, a note is placed,
A melody in silence traced.

Eyes meet in silent serenade,
A thousand dreams in gaze conveyed,
The world falls mute, yet sings within,
A harmony where souls begin.

In quietude, we find our grace,
A tender touch, a gentle space,
Where silence speaks in soft caress,
And hearts in hush find happiness.

The music in the stillness grows,
In silent love, our spirit shows,
A symphony that time suspends,
In harmonies where silence blends.

Savoring Silences

In the hush of dawn's embrace,
Where the whispers softly lie,
Find a world of hidden grace,
Beneath the silent sky.

Quiet moments, gently spoken,
Language of the unseen,
Hearts that mend when softly broken,
In the spaces in between.

Nature's softly drawn refrain,
Birds that sing yet never scream,
In the twilight's gentle gain,
Savor silence, live the dream.

In between each breath we take,
In the quiet's tender fold,
Dreams that stir, a dawn to wake,
Stories in the silence told.

'Round the edges of our fears,
In the silence, wisdom waits,
Listening to a world that hears,
Savoring our whispered fates.

Tiny Triumphs

A child's first steps, a cautious leap,
A heart that dares to fly,
Moments small, but oh so deep,
Triumphs reaching for the sky.

A smile in times of shadows cast,
A light within the night,
Little victories built to last,
Fueling our inner light.

A hand that reaches, finds its grip,
Overcoming, standing tall,
Tiny wins on this life's trip,
Echo grander than a hall.

Daily battles, quietly fought,
Strength in simple gest,
In the smallest, yet most sought,
Finds a triumph manifest.

With every small and steady gain,
With every challenge met,
Tiny triumphs soothe the pain,
In every heart offset.

Poetry in the Ordinary

In the hum of busy streets,
In the thrum of daily life,
There lies a poem, bold yet sweet,
In moments free of strife.

In the flicker of a smile,
Shared in passing glances brief,
In the pauses, all worthwhile,
Lies a solace, a relief.

In the morning's steaming brew,
In the evening's silent dusk,
Poetry in every view,
In the ordinary's husk.

In the hand that holds a pen,
In the voice that speaks a truth,
Every day, and now and then,
Poetry slips through the roof.

In the common and mundane,
Find the verses, hear the song,
Poetry without the strain,
In the rhythm, life belongs.

Magic in the Mundane

In the sweep of broom on floor,
Dust begins its subtle dance,
In each chore a hidden lore,
Given half a chance.

Through the winding of a clock,
Time breathes out its ancient tide,
In each tick a secret knock,
Mysteries that therein hide.

In the folding of the sheets,
Lines of care are drawn anew,
In each act the heart repeats,
Magic in the simplest view.

In the simmer of the stew,
In the stitching's gentle glide,
Wondrous feats in common do,
In the mundane, it resides.

See the wonder, see the grace,
In the tasks that never fade,
Magic in the commonplace,
Every movement, spell conveyed.

Little Miracles

In the dew on morning grass,
There lies a secret held so fast,
Tiny pearls in sunlight's glance,
Nature's whispered, subtle dance.

A bird's call with a rising sun,
Signals a day that's just begun,
Miracles in each small song,
A rhythm where we all belong.

The flicker of a firefly,
Signals hope from earth to sky,
In its glow, a message clear,
Miracles are always near.

A child's laugh in summer's breeze,
Echoes through the swaying trees,
Innocence and joy combined,
Miracles of the purist kind.

In the heartbeats that we share,
Lies a miracle so rare,
In every breath, a sacred gift,
Little miracles our spirits lift.

Delightful Fragments

Scattered petals on the breeze,
Whispers from the ancient trees,
Secrets in the blossoms' fall,
Silent stories nature calls.

Pebbles on a sandy shore,
Each a tale of ages o'er,
Fragments of the ocean's past,
Memories in their edges cast.

Sunbeams through a window pane,
Casting patterns, wild and plain,
Delightful fragments, light's embrace,
Capturing a fleeting grace.

Laughter in a crowded room,
Banishing the deepest gloom,
Moments of pure, shared delight,
Fragments of a timeless night.

In the twinkle of an eye,
In a breath, we may not sigh,
Life reveals its secret parts,
Delightful fragments fill our hearts.

Snippets of Bliss

A smile exchanged in passing glance,
A simple touch, a sweet romance,
In myriad forms, joy exists,
Life is made of blissful snippets.

A melody on evening air,
A moment free from worry, care,
Sublime notes in fleeting time,
Snippets of pure bliss align.

The scent of rain on summer earth,
Nature's gift, a fragrant birth,
In its essence, moments hold,
Blissful snippets, pure and bold.

A whispered word, its meaning clear,
Carrying love for one so dear,
In its sound, a world reveals,
Bliss in snippets life conceals.

In sunlit rays, in moonlit nights,
In the gentle, soothing sights,
Snippets of bliss woven fine,
Within the threads of life's grand design.

Chasing the Small Wonders

In the flutter of a leaf,
In its dance, so brief,
We chase the wonders barely seen,
In moments painted quick and keen.

In the sparkle of a stream,
In the echoes of a dream,
Small wonders carried by the flow,
Chased by hearts that wish to know.

In the brush of morning's gold,
In the stories dew has told,
Chasing wonders, though they fade,
In each dawn, our hopes are laid.

In the laughter of a child,
In the wild and the beguiled,
Small wonders fill the open air,
Chasing them, a breathless affair.

In the quiet of the night,
Beneath the stars' soft light,
Small wonders catch our sighs,
Chasing them is life's surprise.

Blossoms in the Rain

Petals dance on gentle streams,
Nature's whisper soft as dreams.
Raindrops paint the earth so bright,
In the silver kiss of night.

Colors bloom in liquid light,
Grace and beauty through the night.
Silent echoes of the sky,
Blossoms serenely reply.

Threads of dew on tender leaves,
Fluttering in morning's eaves.
Every drop a soothing balm,
In the rain, a peaceful calm.

Gentle winds caress the air,
Fragrance blooms beyond compare.
Garden kissed by tears of skies,
In the rain, each flower sighs.

Spring's embrace in every drop,
Nature's cycle never stops.
Blossoms whisper tales untold,
Raindrops weave a tapestry bold.

Pastel Dreams

Hues of dawn in morning's light,
Pastel dreams take wondrous flight.
Soft as whispers on a breeze,
Color's charm with gentle ease.

Clouds that paint a sky of cream,
Mingle softly with a dream.
Lavender and blush entwine,
Pastel visions so refine.

Fairy tales in colors spun,
Every moment just begun.
Blush of roses, skies so blue,
Pastel dreams come into view.

Gentle palettes, soft and meek,
In their presence, solace seek.
Harbingers of peace and grace,
Dreams unfold in tender space.

In the twilight, dusk's embrace,
Pastels paint a sacred place.
Whispered tones in slumber's gleam,
Hold the essence of a dream.

Heartbeat of the Quiet

Silence dances through the trees,
Whispering in quiet pleas.
Nature's heartbeat, soft and true,
In the stillness, dreams renew.

Gentle murmurs of the night,
Stars that whisper, pure delight.
Breath of wind and sigh of leaves,
All the heart's kind weave.

Echoes carried on the breeze,
Melodies of tranquil seas.
Symphonies of peace unmeasured,
In the stillness, deeply treasured.

Moments linger, time so slow,
In the quiet, rivers flow.
Heartbeats soft, a steady guide,
In the stillness, love resides.

Every pause, a sacred sound,
In the quiet, solace found.
Heartbeat steady, pure and true,
Guides the soul with wisdom's hue.

Songs of Stillness

Whispers in the morning dew,
Harmonies both old and new.
Songs of stillness, soft and pure,
Nature's lullaby, so sure.

Waves that kiss the silent shore,
Echoes from the ocean's core.
Melodies in quiet air,
Gentle songs beyond compare.

Leaves that tremble in the breeze,
Nature's music, life's appease.
Every note a tender thread,
Woven in a calming spread.

Stars that twinkle in the night,
Silent songs, a soft delight.
Every twinkle sings a tune,
Underneath the gentle moon.

In the stillness, find the song,
Harmony where hearts belong.
Songs of peace, of hope, of grace,
In the quiet, find your place.

Whispers in the Breeze

A gentle voice in rustling leaves,
Soft secrets shared with swaying trees,
A story told in nature's tongue,
Where wild and tame in chorus sung.

Through meadows wide and forests deep,
The whispers travel, secrets keep,
From dawn till dusk, a serenade,
In every shadow, light and shade.

A symphony of silent sound,
In every gust, dreams are found,
The wind, a poet, tales it weaves,
In whispers floating on the breeze.

Beneath the stars, beneath the moon,
A nighttime hymn, a soft, sweet tune,
The world in slumber, nature wakes,
In whispers, all the silence breaks.

So listen close, to nature's plea,
In every leaf on every tree,
A whisper calls, a breeze anew,
And nature's song is sung for you.

Moments of Sunshine

A golden ray breaks through the mist,
With tender warmth, the morning kissed,
Soft light that dances on the stream,
Turns every ripple to a dream.

Through windows, shades, and open doors,
A touch of sun on polished floors,
In moments brief, a timeless spark,
A beacon shining in the dark.

In gardens bright, the flowers bloom,
Each petal painted by the noon,
The sunshine whispers through the leaves,
A lullaby the heart receives.

On quiet paths with shadows long,
The sunlit moments, fleeting, strong,
A fleeting brush of pure delight,
In every corner, soft and bright.

So take these moments, pure and free,
And let them linger, let them be,
For sunshine holds a world so bright,
In moments fleeting, pure as light.

Petals in the Morning

Awake with dawn, a new day born,
The flowers greet the early morn,
Each petal soaked in dew's embrace,
A picture painted with such grace.

The colors bloom beneath the sun,
A dance of light as day's begun,
With every breeze, they softly sway,
In gentle tones of pink and gray.

The garden hums a morning song,
Where petals find where they belong,
In harmony with nature's call,
A living tapestry for all.

In every shade, a story grows,
As morning's light on petals shows,
The beauty in each flower's croon,
A melody that ends too soon.

So cherish moments, calm and clear,
When petals wake and day is near,
For morning whispers in the flowers,
Are nature's gentle, fleeting hours.

Dew-kissed Smiles

In morning light, the world awakes,
With dew-kissed smiles as day breaks,
The leaves adorned in crystal glow,
A fleeting touch from dawn's first show.

The meadows gleam with drops of light,
A thousand diamonds in plain sight,
Each blade of grass a canvas bright,
In morning's calm, a sweet delight.

The flowers stretch with yawns of gold,
Their petals shimmer, soft and bold,
Dew-kissed in silent, tender grace,
A smile that lights up every space.

In quiet moments, pure and still,
The dew descends with gentle will,
A kiss from night to greet the day,
A smile that chases dark away.

So pause and breathe in morning's cheer,
With dew-kissed smiles so bright and clear,
For in each drop, a world anew,
A whispered joy, a radiant view.

Inklings of Bliss

In twilight's tender, soft embrace,
A whisper of joy begins to trace,
Through leaves that shimmer, softly sway,
Inklings of bliss at the close of day.

A bird's sweet song, a melody bright,
Echoes gently through the night,
Soothing murmurs, a serene kiss,
On restless hearts, inklings of bliss.

Stars emerge, a glittering veil,
With stories of old they softly exhale,
Silver threads in the velvet abyss,
Weaving dreams, inklings of bliss.

Moonlight spills on sleeping trees,
A tranquil dance with night's cool breeze,
Caressing branches, a gentle miss,
Nature's art, inklings of bliss.

Eyes close softly, hearts now rest,
In the quiet we find our best,
Lulled by the night's gentle abyss,
Cradled in inklings of pure bliss.

Quiet Elations

Morning light with tender touch,
Wakes the world, a gentle hush,
Golden beams through windowpanes,
Quiet elations in soft refrains.

Petals open, dewdrops gleam,
In the dawn's first hopeful beam,
Each glistening drop, a silent cheer,
Quiet elations, pure and clear.

Butterflies in whispered flight,
Dance with the breeze in morning light,
Soft as feathers, they glide and twist,
Whispers of quiet, tender bliss.

Streams that babble, soft and low,
Over pebbles, gentle and slow,
Their song a lullaby, nature's tune,
Quiet elations, a soft croon.

Hearts find peace in moments small,
Amidst the dawn, nature's call,
In every breath, a soft salvation,
Found in quiet elations.

Silent Radiances

Twinkling stars in night's embrace,
Amidst the sky, they softly trace,
Silent lights in the vast expanse,
Radiances in silent dance.

Moon's soft glow, a silver tear,
Falls on earth, serene and clear,
Its beams of light, a quiet trance,
Gifting us silent radiance.

Snowflakes kiss the ground so light,
In the stillness of the night,
Each one a gem in winter's glance,
Silent radiances, nature's prance.

Lanterns lit in gardens fair,
Casting glows on evening air,
Their gentle flames in shadows prance,
Creating silent radiance.

Hearts that meet with kindness pure,
A grace that shines forevermore,
In every smile, in every chance,
Lives a silent radiance.

Whispers of Warmth

In autumn's golden, crisp embrace,
Leaves descend with gentle grace,
Each fluttered fall a softened charm,
Whispers of warmth, a quiet calm.

Fireside embers softly gleam,
Casting shadows in a dream,
Crackling whispers that disarm,
Fill the heart with whispers warm.

Hands entwined on a winter's day,
Walking through the snow's soft sway,
Each touch a promise to keep from harm,
In shared whispers of warmth so warm.

Blankets draped in evening's hush,
Comfort found without the rush,
Sighs of peace in night's sweet balm,
Resting in whispers of warm calm.

Memories held in tender keep,
Lull the soul to dreams so deep,
In the heart's chamber, far from storm,
Lie whispers of enduring warmth.

Crickets' Serenade

In twilight's whisper, shadows creep,
Crickets' song, the night does keep.
A gentle hum, a timeless tune,
Underneath the watchful moon.

Leaves dance to rhythmic serenade,
In grass and grove, their song is laid.
Stars above, in silent applause,
Witness to night's soothing cause.

Through night's embrace, whispers flow,
Dreams alight, in crickets' glow.
Soft and steady, pure and true,
A melody born of evening dew.

Nature's chorus, rich and sweet,
In the dark, hearts gently meet.
Every note a precious thread,
In this nightly, woven spread.

Till dawn breaks with golden light,
Crickets fade into the night.
Their hymn, a memory saved,
In the book of twilight's crave.

Pebbles of Time

On the shore of endless days,
Pebbles whisper in soft displays.
Shaped by waves and fleeting hours,
Time's handiwork, its subtle powers.

Each pebble tells a hidden lore,
Ancient tales of yesteryore.
Carved by moments, smooth and worn,
In silence, histories are borne.

Casting dreams upon the sea,
Past and present, wild and free.
Currents swirl and tides do change,
In their dance, they re-arrange.

Collect the pebbles, one by one,
Underneath the setting sun.
Time as fleeting as a sigh,
Yet in stones, it will abide.

Pebbles gathered, tales encased,
Memories etched, yet never erased.
In their presence, we find grace,
Pieces of time we can't replace.

Tranquil Reflections

Upon a still and mirror'd lake,
Dreams of past and future wake.
Silent ripples spread and fade,
In peace, the heart is unafraid.

Mountains tall, their shadows fall,
Reflected in the tranquil thrall.
Whispers of the forest near,
Echo softly, calm and clear.

Birds above in graceful flight,
Marry day with coming night.
In their arcs, a silent song,
Where peace and stillness both belong.

Moments linger, breath held tight,
Softly kissed by twilight's light.
In reflections vast and deep,
Whispered secrets safely keep.

Nature's canvas, still and bright,
Captures essence, pure and light.
In these waters, calm and clear,
Find the peace that draws you near.

Simplicity's Symphony

In quiet fields where daisies grow,
Simplicity's sweet breezes blow.
Nature hums a gentle tune,
Beneath the sun, the stars, the moon.

Children play in meadows wide,
Innocence their only guide.
Running through the golden grain,
Unaware of life's refrain.

Streams that babble, soft and clear,
Sing of joy and quiet cheer.
In their flow, we find our song,
Simple, sweet, where hearts belong.

In the woods, the trees stand tall,
Whispering secrets, soft and small.
Leaves that rustle, winds that play,
Compose the music of the day.

Life in simplest forms expressed,
In this beauty, we are blessed.
Symphony of pure delight,
Peace and joy in every sight.

Raindrops on Leaves

Raindrops dance on verdant leaves,
A symphony of gentle grieves.
Each tiny drop, a world of light,
Glittering in the twilight.

Nature's tears, in silence fall,
Answering the forest's call.
They quench the thirst of earth's embrace,
Leaving trails of liquid grace.

Emerald crowns with silver jewels,
In the showers, nature cools.
Ripples form on puddles small,
Echoing a distant call.

Whispers of the stormy air,
Leaves in wind, without a care.
Every drop, a song to sing,
In the hush of rain's soft ring.

Come dawn's light, the rains desist,
Leaves adorned in morning mist.
Nature's gems in silver chains,
Heaven's gift as peace remains.

Butterfly Ballet

In the garden, petals light,
Butterflies take airy flight.
Graceful wings in colors bright,
Dancing in the morning light.

Pirouettes on zephyrs' glide,
A ballet neither forced nor tied.
In each flutter, heartbeats merge,
Nature's rhythm, gentle surge.

Soft they land on blooming rose,
Whisper secrets wind bestows.
Ecstasy in patterns sewn,
Life's brief beauty, brightly shown.

In the sunbeam, joyous gleam,
Butterflies craft dreams from dream.
Their fleeting dance, a whispered song,
Nature's art, where we belong.

Silent dancers, fleeting grace,
In their flight, we find our place.
Ephemeral yet deeply real,
In this ballet, we both heal.

Secrets of the Meadow

Meadow whispers in the breeze,
Secrets hidden 'neath the trees.
Wildflowers tell tales of old,
In the dusk, their stories fold.

Grasses sway and murmurs rise,
Underneath the endless skies.
Each rustling leaf, a word to share,
Meadow's lore beyond compare.

Buttercups and clover sweet,
Hold the earth in quiet greet.
Whispers woven in the blades,
Love's old tunes in light cascades.

Beneath the moon and starry dome,
Meadow keeps her tales at home.
Crickets sing their nightly tune,
Echoes of the sun and moon.

Dawn will come and light will play,
But secrets of the night will stay.
In the meadows, whispers keep,
Nature's voice in silence deep.

Daily Blessings

The morning sun peeks from above,
With warmth and light, a gift of love,
Birds serenade the break of dawn,
Another day, life marches on.

With every breath, a silent prayer,
In moments still beyond compare,
Grateful hearts in simple things,
Unseen joy that each day brings.

The scent of flowers in the air,
Children's laughter, worries rare,
Nature's canvas, a moving sight,
Daily blessings, pure delight.

Shared meals with friends who care,
Soft whispers in the evening air,
Candles flicker, thoughts unwind,
In these moments, solace find.

Tides of twilight, stars arise,
Night embraces, gentle skies,
Sleep in peace, tomorrow's plea,
Daily blessings set us free.

Luminous Flecks

Midnight sky with twinkling stars,
Whispers tales of worlds afar,
Luminous flecks in velvet night,
Guiding souls with gentle light.

Moonlight dances on the sea,
Waves of dreams, tranquility,
In the depths of silent dark,
Hope ignites a tiny spark.

Fireflies in a summer's eve,
Hearts entwined, we dare believe,
Magic fills the balmy air,
Luminous flecks beyond compare.

In the shadow and the gleam,
Moments paint a living dream,
Embers glow where love protects,
Life adorned with luminous flecks.

Daybreak comes, the sky complies,
Morning dew in soft reprise,
Luminous flecks fade in light,
Memories lingering, pure and bright.

Sprinkled Laughter

Children's giggles, pure and free,
Echoing through the whispering trees,
Sprinkled laughter, bright and clear,
Innocence, our hearts endear.

Joyful moments, shared and true,
Like morning sunlight, sparkling dew,
In their eyes, a world anew,
Sprinkled laughter, joy pursue.

Tickles, tales, untamed glee,
Every second, boundless spree,
Time suspended, worries shatter,
In the dance of sprinkled laughter.

Smiles paint the canvas bright,
Spreading warmth, a radiant light,
Echoes linger, ages after,
Treasured sound of sprinkled laughter.

Evening falls, the day concludes,
Silent stars in their solitudes,
Yet our hearts will always gather,
Memories of sprinkled laughter.

Whispers in the Breeze

Gentle zephyrs, soft embrace,
Caressing cheeks with tender grace,
Whispers in the breeze convey,
Secrets of the fleeting day.

Leaves are rustling, stories told,
Natures symphony unfolds,
Invisible hands gently tease,
Life adorned with whispered ease.

Through the meadows, past the streams,
Breezes carry wistful dreams,
Dances swaying, undeterred,
Whispers in the breeze, unheard.

Silent vows beneath the sky,
Echoed by the breeze's sigh,
Lovers' promises, heart's decree,
Captured in the whispering spree.

Night descends with tranquil peace,
Winds slow down, their whispers cease,
Yet the echoes linger, please,
Of those sweet whispers in the breeze.

Micro-Miracles

In the quiet of the dawn,
Mysteries begin to flow.
Tiny miracles are born,
In the spaces we don't know.

Smallest moments take control,
Like the flutter of a wing.
Whispers touch the deepest soul,
Life's simplest, sweetest thing.

Drops of dew like liquid pearls,
Rest upon the morning grass.
Echoes of a hidden world,
In each moment that we pass.

In the silent, gentle nod,
Magic slips between the cracks.
Micro-miracles of God,
Found in life's soft, subtle tracks.

From the opening of a bud,
Through the endless ocean's wave.
Miracles misunderstood,
Every breath we take and gave.

Skies in a Teacup

Pour the tea as days unfold,
In the warmth, a sky decants.
Clouds and dreams in cups of gold,
Whirling through a tiny dance.

Sips become a swirling breeze,
Flavor of the distant stars.
Galaxies within these leaves,
Holding secrets close and far.

Steam ascends like morning mist,
Brushstrokes on a porcelain frame.
In this moment, we exist,
As vast worlds we softly name.

Ripples form in tranquil pools,
Glimpses of the infinite.
Boundless skies in simple rules,
In each teacup, cosmos lit.

With each sip, horizons blend,
Worlds within, upon our lips.
Infinites we can pretend,
In these skies where teacup sips.

Whispers of a Smile

Caught within a fleeting glance,
Whispers of a smile bloom.
Soft enchantment of a chance,
Lighting up a darkened room.

Curves of joy that softly bend,
Bridges made with gentle grace.
In that moment eyes extend,
Heart to heart, we find our place.

Silent language brightly spun,
Spoken through a tender look.
Every smile a setting sun,
With a warmth that no one took.

Messages in silent cheer,
Words unneeded, truth revealed.
Whispers found, forever near,
Power of a smile healed.

In the quiet of a grin,
Worlds are crafted, tales entwine.
Whispers of a smile within,
Touch the soul with light divine.

The Beauty of Now

Seconds dance between our breaths,
Moments shaped in present tense.
Life unveils in subtle depths,
Beauty found in every sense.

Now is where the heart resides,
In the blink of fleeting time.
In this space where joy abides,
Every beat becomes a rhyme.

Present holds a boundless key,
Unlocking realms of pure delight.
Endless possibilities,
In the soft and tender light.

Each experience we tread,
Is a canvas bright and clear.
Painted in an instant's spread,
Beauty of the now, sincere.

Treasure each and every beat,
For the now is all we know.
Moments cherished, lives complete,
In the present's gentle flow.

Soft Gleams

In twilight's tender, muted light,
Soft gleams kiss the silent night,
Whispers of starlight gently beam,
In dreams, we find a sacred theme.

A tranquil breeze through willows weaves,
Dew-kissed fields with shimmering leaves,
Night's hush invites a world serene,
Bathe in the glow of a moonlit scene.

Reflections dance on waters clear,
Soft magic sparkles, drawing near,
In nature's calm, our spirits blend,
On gentle waves, all troubles mend.

Golden hues at dawn break free,
Heralding the day with serenity,
Soft gleams ignite a hopeful start,
Lighting the path within our heart.

Day's journey ends as night descends,
Soft gleams of dusk, our silent friends,
Embrace the calm, let worries stream,
In stardust, find your sweetest dream.

Unfolding Joy

In petals bright, joy begins,
With morning light, the day spins,
A world anew in colors grand,
Unfolding joy with nature's hand.

Each bloom a smile in sun's embrace,
Pure happiness in every face,
Hearts open wide to life's sweet song,
Where moments of bliss gently throng.

Laughter echoes through the air,
A melody beyond compare,
With every breath, a pure delight,
Unfolding joy shines day and night.

The golden warmth of friendships dear,
Moments cherished, year by year,
Togetherness in simple things,
Joy unfurls with every spring.

Beneath the sky of endless blue,
In little things, find something true,
Unfolding joy in life's sweet dance,
In each small moment, take a chance.

Petite Pleasures

A dewdrop gleams, a morning kiss,
Nature's charms in moments missed,
Small delights in every view,
Petite pleasures, pure and true.

The rustle of leaves, a gentle breeze,
The soft hum of bees in trees,
In tiny wonders, hearts find peace,
Life's simple joys that never cease.

A child's laugh, a warm embrace,
The tender touch of love's grace,
In fleeting whispers, life's refrain,
Echoes the joy in small domains.

The taste of rain on summer's eve,
The marvel of what we believe,
In those petite, sweet treasures found,
Joy in small delights abound.

On winding paths through fields of green,
In moments quiet and serene,
Petite pleasures, a breath of spring,
The simple joys that life can bring.

Reveling in the Minute

A single leaf upon the ground,
Autumn whispers, soft and sound,
In moments still, the world seems bright,
Reveling in the minute light.

A fleeting glance, a knowing smile,
An extra mile, walked for a while,
In every heartbeat, joy concealed,
Minute wonders, slow revealed.

A bird in flight, a silent stream,
Life's harmony in nature's theme,
In pauses brief, we catch a view,
Minute marvels, old and new.

The tick of clocks, a passing glance,
A sunbeam's dance in whispered trance,
In fragments small, the grandeur lies,
Reveling in the minute skies.

Between the dawn and dusk's swift fall,
In every breath, we find it all,
Reveling in the minute's grace,
Life's unfurling, a warm embrace.

Milton Keynes UK
Ingram Content Group UK Ltd.
UKHW022119220724
445848UK00012B/181

9 789916 763216